Under a Parrot Sky

illustrated by
Luisa Uribe

written by
Rachel Delahaye

RISING ★ STARS

ISBN: 9781510445000

Text, design, illustrations and layout © 2017 Hodder and Stoughton Ltd
First published in 2017 by Rising Stars, part of Hodder Education Group
An Hachette UK Company
Carmelite House, 50 Victoria Embankment, London EC4Y 0DZ

www.risingstars-uk.com

Impression number 10 9 8
Year 2025 2024 2023 202

Author: Rachel Delahaye
Series Editor: Sasha Mort(
Senior Publisher: Helen Pa
Illustrator: Luisa Uribe
Educational Consultant: P
Design concept: Julie Jou
Page layout: Steve Evans
Editorial: Stephanie Matth

Thanks to Beata Høst and

With thanks to the schools
including: Ancaster CE Prim
Ferry Lane Primary School, London; Foxborough Primary School, Slough; Griffin Park
Primary School, Blackburn; St Barnabas CE First & Middle School, Pershore; Tranmoor
Primary School, Doncaster; and Wilton CE Primary School, Wilton.

The right of Rachel Delahaye to be identified as the author of this work has been
asserted by her in accordance with the Copyright, Designs & Patents Act 1988.

A catalogue record for this title is available from the British Library.

Printed in the United Kingdom

Orders: Please contact Hachette UK Distribution, Hely Hutchinson Centre, Milton
Road, Didcot, Oxfordshire, OX11 7HH
Telephone: +44 (0)1235 400555 Email: primary@hachette.co.uk. Lines are open
from 9 a.m. to 5 p.m., Monday to Friday.

MIX
Paper from
responsible sources
FSC
www.fsc.org
FSC™ C104740

 Contents

Chapter 1

Just a minute ago she had seen an army of jellyfish with bright colours and deadly stingers, and now she was face to face with a giant hippo! Lily stared at the picture and imagined herself right there, on the banks of the brown river, watching it for real through her camera lens.

"Is that hippo yawning?" Lily's mother asked, peering closely at the photograph.

"Opening their jaws is a sign of aggression," Lily said. "It says so on the information."

On the information sheet next to the picture, it also said that the photographer was a ten-year-old girl called Asreen. *Lucky Asreen,* thought Lily, *ending up in the finals of the Young Photographer of the Year!* With every photo she'd seen in the exhibition, Lily's desire to be part of it had grown. She had been taking photos and reading books about photography since she was six. Having a photo on display for everyone to admire would be a dream come true.

"Even if it is angry, I think this hippo is my favourite," her mother said.

"Come over here, I'll show you mine!"

Lily ran to a photograph further along the wall. It was a huge parrot in flight, its green and yellow feathers electric against the dark forest background. The photograph was titled, 'Cloak of Colour'.

"It's a great green macaw. The girl who shot it is only 11 years old."

"She shot it?" Lily's mother said, alarmed.

"With a camera, silly!" Lily sighed. "A camera just like mine. I've decided – I'm going to enter the competition next year."

Her mother smiled. "I can see it now … This year's Young Photographer of the Year is … Lily Costas!"

Lily performed a little bow, and her mother clapped.

"Come on, we'd better meet Dad. He's waiting for us in the cafe."

"Why did he leave?" Lily asked.

"I think he got a bit bored after the first hour."

"Bored?" Lily gasped with disbelief. "I could stay here all day and I wouldn't get bored."

Lily's mother laughed. "Come on, let's pick up an entry form for next year's competition on the way out. And we'll buy a postcard or two from the gift shop as souvenirs. We'll get the parrot one, shall we?"

"And the yawning hippo for Dad," Lily said with a naughty grin.

On the way home, Lily daydreamed about a large photograph mounted on a wall in a grand building. It would be bold and bright, and people would crowd around, leaning in to read the information sheet next to it.

Title: _____

Photographer: Liliana Costas, age 11
United Kingdom

Hmm, what would the title be? considered Lily. *It would
have to be exotic-sounding, like 'A Sky of Parrots' or 'A
Paintbox of Flowers' ... Something vibrant and filled with
rainbow colours ...*

At the sound of rain against the car window,
Lily woke from her daydream and looked at the
competition form in her hands. The deadline for
entries was March, just three months away. Her heart

sank. Wind, rain and mud is all that happened before March in the United Kingdom. December, January, February – every single month was dull and grey.

She was about to crumple the paper into a ball when she remembered something. The February school holiday! Her parents had talked about a trip to see Aunty Agda – yes, she'd heard them discussing flight times and whether they could take her out of school for a couple of days. *Aunty Agda didn't live around the corner. She lived somewhere exciting. Where was it again?* wondered Lily. *Oh yes …*

South Africa!

Chapter 2

The engines began to roar as the plane picked up speed. A few more seconds and they'd be taking off. Lily gripped the book in her lap.

A Guide to Birds of South Africa was her favourite possession. It went with her everywhere. She knew every bird in it, from eagles to bee-eaters to sunbirds – and if she could get a photo of a magical lilac-breasted roller, the judges of the Young Photographer of the Year wouldn't be able to resist!

The only trouble was, the plane wasn't going to South Africa.

Instead of flying south towards warmth and colour, Lily was heading north, to a land that was cold and white.

Just four weeks before the trip to South Africa, Lily's parents had received an invitation to talk at a World Geology Conference in Norway. They were both geologists – experts in rock pressure and oil fields – and Lily knew it was really important. But when she'd looked up Norway on the Internet, it looked like a white desert, and it was hard to hide her disappointment. To make things worse, her best friend Olive was going to Australia for two weeks. Australia! She could take a thousand winning photographs in a place like that.

But now she wouldn't even be entering the competition.

What would be the point? she thought. *What was there to see in Norway but snow, snow, snow?*

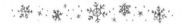

There wasn't a direct flight, so they had to change planes in Norway's capital, Oslo. By the time they landed in Tromsø, it was late at night and Lily was tired.

They were met at the airport by a tall man with a wide smile, who took her hand and shook it roughly.

"I'm Ivan. Welcome to the Land of the Midnight Sun!" he said.

"But I don't see any sun," Lily said.

"Not now, but come back in summertime, and then you will see nothing but sun. It never sets. You're impressed?" Ivan was watching her for a reaction.

Lily smiled and nodded, even though the only thing

that could possibly impress her at that moment would be news that they were getting straight on to a plane to South Africa.

"She is speechless," he declared, clapping his hands. "She can't believe it! I have lots more stories to tell you, but maybe not tonight, hey? Come on, let's get you all tucked up in bed."

"Ivan Larsen works at the Institute for Geoscience," Lily's father explained.

"He's one of the conference organisers, and his family has invited us to stay," Lily's mother said.

"And I have kids, so while your parents are working, you won't be lonely," Ivan added.

As they drove into the night, Lily could see nothing but the eerie blue of snow at night – on the ground, on the rooftops and on the dark, craggy mountains all around. Everything was deadly silent, as if the land had been smothered by a blanket. It felt like the loneliest place on Earth.

Chapter 3

Lily's eyes flickered open.

She was on a sofa-bed in Ivan's study. The night before, she had fallen asleep instantly without knowing or caring where she was. Now, she could see shelves of books about Norway, and tall display cases with glass doors. They were filled with bits of rock and crystal that glistened in the bright sunshine pouring through the window.

Lily got up and opened the study door. There were voices down the corridor. A strange language. A dog barking. Plates rattling on a table. The smells of toast and coffee. Her tummy rumbled. Still in her pyjamas, she headed towards the noise and found herself in the kitchen.

There wasn't a single face she recognised. A boy and a girl sat at the table, and a woman was tidying plates. She stopped when she saw Lily.

"Hello, sleepy head!" she said. "*Kom og sett deg*. Come and sit." Her voice was funny and delicate.

"I am Linn, and this is Morten and this is Asta."
She smiled. "Morten is 16 but Asta I think is your age, 12, yes?"

"I'm 11, nearly 12," Lily said, trying not to panic. Where were her parents? "Nice to meet you. Is my mum here?"

"They have all gone to work already. You are sleeping very late! We are finished breakfast, but there is coffee and toast and jam for you. Asta, please help our guest."

Linn's voice rose and fell like a lullaby; it was sweet and friendly. The children were not. Morten smiled only briefly before looking back at his phone, and from the look on Asta's sour face, helping the guest was the last thing she wanted to do.

"Coffee?" Asta said unsmiling.

"No thank you. I don't drink coffee."

Under the table, something tickled Lily's legs and she shrieked.

"*Stikk, Bodil!*" Linn shouted. "*Stikk!*"

Linn shooed Bodil, a large brown and white husky, out of the room. Lily saw Morten coax him back in with food under the table.

"When will my parents be back?"

Linn shrugged. "When they finish looking at rocks. They think they are rock stars!"

"She always says that joke," Morten said, shaking his head.

Lily tried to hold back her tears. She didn't know these people, and although they spoke good English, it was all strange. She felt lost.

"What am I going to do today?" she asked.

"Well, you are going to be a Norwegian child."

"H-how?"

Linn smiled. "First, you learn how to ski. Morten and Asta will show you how."

Asta let out a huge sigh and skulked out of the room, slamming the door behind her.

"Asta! *Kom hit!*" Linn called. "Come here!" she said again. The girl didn't return. "I am sorry. She is not happy at the moment. We give her some time, okay?"

That's two of us who aren't happy, Lily thought.

Lily was told to take ski clothes from the cupboard. Remembering the cold snow, she wrapped herself in so many layers she could barely move. Right outside the back door, there was a rack – a bit like a bicycle rack – that held long skis. Morten was further down the garden, already wearing his. Asta appeared and slipped hers on quickly and expertly, and glided towards Morten. She stopped and looked back.

"Morten! Morten! *Kom hit!*" she called, pointing at Lily.

When Morten saw Lily's outfit, he laughed so hard she wished the snow would swallow her up.

"Here in Tromsø, the weather is never so bad," Morten

explained, still spluttering. "You will boil like a coffee pot. You should take off some layers."

Lily went inside and returned wearing just one warm jacket, ski trousers and gloves. Morten was right – it wasn't that cold, or maybe she was just still hot with embarrassment. Linn arrived, looking elegant in a red all-in-one ski suit. She was holding boots.

"These should be the right size for you."

Lily stood still as Linn tightened them. She looked up and around at the mountains.

"How do we get up there?" She pointed at the peaks.

"You are kidding me!" Morten said. "You are not going up there. You are learning to ski in the garden like a baby."

"He means beginner," Linn tutted. "There is always a hold up between languages."

"It's called a language barrier," Lily said.

Her parents had told her about it – how the choice of words in one language can create a misunderstanding in another. Even so, she felt her eyes sting with unfairness. Language barrier or not, the Larsen children were cruel. Linn seemed to be the only friendly person around.

"These skis are funny," Lily said.

"They are cross-country skis. Much longer and thinner than downhill skis. The boots are different, too. Can you see how the heel lifts up? It's so you can ski like you are walking. Morten, show Lily."

Morten skied down the garden and back again. He made it look so easy.

"Your turn," he said.

Lily gripped on to Linn's arm.

"When you want to stop, turn the tops of the skis inwards to make an upside-down V shape," Linn said, demonstrating. "Be brave now."

Linn peeled Lily's fingers away from her arm; immediately, Lily's feet slipped forwards. She made windmill movements with her arms as she tried to keep her balance. Morten laughed at her again, but she tried to ignore him. She bent her knees, thinking it would keep her steady, but it made her go faster. As she picked up speed she started to scream.

"Do a V shape," Linn called, so Lily angled her feet as she was shown.

But instead of coming to a gentle stop, the tips of the skis crossed over and crashed together. She tripped and fell.

"You have no control," Morten said, shaking his head.

"Let's go for a trek," Linn said. "You will get used to it."

Asta sighed heavily. "I stay home."

Linn paused and then nodded. "Do you mind?" she asked Lily.

Lily didn't mind at all. She and Asta were obviously never going to be friends.

Chapter 4

With Linn by her side, Lily made it down the long garden. Morten showed off his side-to-side skiing, called 'herringbone'; Linn said 'duckwalk' was a better description. It was too difficult for a beginner, but Lily was getting used to her skis. She could keep them both pointing forwards, at least!

At the bottom of the garden they went through a gate and on to a path into thick woods. The snowy forest floor was criss-crossed with ski tracks.

"Follow the tracks. It's easier that way," Linn said, slotting her own skis into the grooves.

Lily copied, and soon she began to get into a good rhythm.

"I think you are a Norwegian girl now!" Linn sang.

"*Yeg er Norsk*," Morten said. "It means 'I am Norwegian'. Say it: *Yeg er Norsk*."

"*Yeg er Norsk*," Lily called back.

"Remember, when you spell '*Yeg*' it starts with the letter 'j'. Jeg," Linn said.

"Mamma, she's not at school!" Morten said. "Come on, Norsk girl, let's race. I'll give you a head start. Go!"

Lily laughed nervously and pushed ahead, leaving Linn and Morten behind.

And that's when it happened.

At first, it was just a sound – a whooshing and clinking. She thought it was Morten catching up with her, but then a large group of men burst through the trees up ahead. They were wearing racing suits with numbers on their fronts. Their breath burst from their mouths in short cloudy puffs.

"Lily, stop!" Linn's voice warned from far behind.

But Lily couldn't stop. She was going fast now, skis tucked inside the tracks. She tried to change direction, but the skis were long and heavy – they wouldn't go where she wanted them to go … and … CRASH.

Some of the skiers jumped sideways, but most of them fell over her or crashed into each other. There were skis and men scattered everywhere.

"Sorry, sorry," was all Lily could say. But sorry wasn't good enough. The men were angry. They shook their heads and they shouted.

She hated this place. Hated it!

On her bed in the Larsens' study, Lily held *A Guide to Birds of South Africa* against her chest and sobbed. It wasn't fair. South Africa was going to be the holiday of her dreams, and now she was on a nightmare trip where everything was going wrong. The study door opened.

Lily leaped up and wrapped her arms around her mother's waist.

"I want to go home. Please, please, can we go?"

Lily's mother sat her back down on the edge of the bed. "So you tripped up the Tromsø Men's Cross-Country Ski Championship … No big deal."

Her mother was trying to make her laugh, but it only made Lily more upset.

"It's not your fault," her mother soothed. "They often have races through the forest, and Linn says she was silly to take you there without checking first. Besides," she added, lifting Lily's chin. "Those skiers now have a very funny story to tell their families!"

"They weren't laughing," Lily sniffed. "They were really angry."

"Maybe they won't laugh today, but one day they will. And so will you, when you get your sense of humour back." She winked.

Linn appeared in the doorway. "Come on, my champion tripper," she said. "We have the fire on in the living room, and you must try *gløgg* – it is hot apple juice with spices. You will like it."

Lily shook her head and buried it in her pillow.

"I think it's been a big day," Lily's mother explained.

"Asta isn't feeling well, either," Linn said.

"Everything will be better in the morning," said Lily's mother. "You'll see."

Lily doubted that very much.

Chapter 5

When Lily woke, every single muscle in her body ached – her legs and arms, and even her hips. She hobbled into the kitchen where everyone apart from Asta was already seated for breakfast.

"Aha!" Ivan said with a big smile. "Cross-country skiing is a workout, yes?"

Lily nodded. "Pretty painful."

"Well, the good news is – you are strong enough to live in Norway," he said. "You have to be tough to live here, and you were tough enough to stop a whole race!" He laughed loudly and Lily felt her face go hot.

"Ivan …" Linn tutted. "Don't tease."

"No, no. It's just for fun," Ivan said. "Come, Lily, you must be hungry, and you're in time for a full breakfast today. There is yoghurt, toast, cheese, fish, coffee …"

He gestured to the table with its strange selection of foods. Lily asked for plain toast.

"Suit yourself," Ivan said, tipping smoked fish on to his own plate.

"Will you check on Asta?" Linn said to Morten. "Ask her if she will come and join us today. Perhaps we can go trekking."

"Does she have a temperature?" Lily's mother asked.

"She's not ill," Linn said, pouring steaming hot coffee into Lily's cup without asking. "Her puppy ran away." She pointed to a photograph on the wall. It was Asta with a tiny, beautiful grey and white dog – a heart-shaped mark on its head.

"She has to get over it," Ivan said impatiently. "What about *skikjøring*?"

Linn shrugged. The atmosphere was a bit tense, so Lily sipped coffee for something to do. It was strong and bitter.

"What is *skikjøring*?" Lily's mother asked.

"It means 'ski driving'. Asta ties a dog to her belt and the dog pulls her on skis – fast! She is very good." For a moment Ivan looked proud, but then his face fell. "She is getting all silly about the dog and forgetting there is an important race in a couple of days."

"It sounds very exciting," Lily said, trying to make conversation.

"Maybe you would like to try it?" Ivan said, brightening.

Lily nearly choked. "No. No thank you!"

Ivan, Linn and her parents laughed.

"So, what do you want to do today, Lily?" Linn asked.

"Nothing." Lily wasn't ready to put skis on again, and what else was there to do here?

Morten returned with a big sigh. "Asta says she wants to stay home."

Ivan slammed the table with both fists. "Two girls who don't want to do anything. Ridiculous! Come on, Costas, we need to go."

Lily was shaken by Ivan's outburst and tried not to cry as she watched her mother and father getting their work things together.

"Don't worry," Morten whispered, nodding towards his father. "He is not cross. He just likes to get people moving. He is a kind of action man! He doesn't like laziness."

"I'm not lazy. I'm just not feeling well." Lily pretended to sneeze and ran to the study.

People with strange manners, fish for breakfast, nothing but snow and more snow! This place was the worst! She grabbed her bird book and sat at the desk by the window in a patch of warm sun. She closed her eyes and imagined she was somewhere with friendly people and tropical fruit breakfasts. When she opened her eyes, her mother was standing in front of her.

"Why don't you go out with your camera today?"

"There's nothing to photograph."

"Nothing?" Lily's mother put her hands on her hips. Her patience was running out. "Tell me, Lily, which photograph won this year's competition?"

Lily remembered the ones she liked – the bird, the jellyfish, the clownfish, the monkey eating the flower. They were all finalists, but they didn't win the big prize. She realised she had never found out which photo did.

"I'll tell you, shall I?" her mother said. "It was a picture of some fishermen pulling clams from the sand. Taken on a beach in England."

"Clams? England?"

"Yes, and they weren't even pretty clams, or pretty fishermen! Sometimes it isn't the show-stoppers that stop the show, but a fresh look at life around us."

Lily looked back at her bird book – a white-fronted bee-eater on the cover with plumes of red, green and yellow. Could something ordinary really beat something so beautiful?

"Tell you what, if I let you speak to Olive, will you promise to cheer up?"

"Olive, really?"

"It's bedtime in Australia, but you might just catch her before she goes to sleep. Here, you can use my phone."

"Thanks, Mum." Lily took the phone and dialled her friend on video chat.

"Hello?" A bleary face peered into the camera.

"Olive, it's me, Lily!"

"Hey Lily. How's Norway?"

"It's cold and boring. I don't even want to talk about it. What have you been doing?"

"Just sitting by the pool. We went shopping, too."

Lily noticed she was wearing vest pyjamas because of the heat. A million miles away from snow and ice.

"Have you seen any wildlife yet?"

"Dad and Luke went on some snorkelling trip, but I couldn't be bothered."

"What do you mean?" Lily was shocked. *Why wouldn't anyone want to go snorkelling?* Even in the shallows there were parrot fish and urchins and mother-of-pearl shells.

"The sun's out, and there's a beach and a swimming pool. What else do I need?"

"Seahorses and stripy fish!"

"I can see those in an aquarium, any time."

"What about the koalas and kangaroos?"

"Wildlife and adventure is your thing, Lily, not mine."

"But how do you know if it's not your thing unless you try it?"

"Are you doing anything good in Norway today?"

"No. It's boring."

"If you're not going to try anything new, then why should I?"

Chapter 6

The house was quiet. Lily's parents had gone with Ivan back to the conference, Morten was out skiing with friends, and Linn was in the living room working at a computer. Asta, as usual, was in her room.

Lily cast her eye along the bookshelves in the study. She took one called *Wild Norway* to the kitchen table and poured herself some coffee. The taste was still strange, but it made her feel awake. And it was definitely time to wake up, she'd decided. Olive could be unadventurous if she wanted to be, but Olive wasn't an adventurer or a photographer. What sort of photographer would Lily be if she didn't explore her surroundings?

It turned out that *Wild Norway* was a wonderful book. Lily didn't realise that there were rabbits, foxes, reindeer and elk. Even bears! All the animals were mainly white or brown for camouflage, but they were still beautiful. She especially liked the elk with their majestic antlers. The book said they were hard to spot

but locals could often tell you which areas they were last seen in. She would ask Linn.

Linn was on a phone call and Lily didn't want to disturb her. The only other person in the house was Asta. Asta's room was the last place Lily wanted to go, but today was the day of being brave, so she knocked softly on her door.

There was a nose-blowing noise. Then: "*Ja?*"

Asta was sitting on her bed, holding a photograph of a dog.

"Is that the puppy?" Lily asked gently, stepping forwards.

"Yes, it's Luna."

Lily had come to ask about elk, but there was a sadness in Asta's face. Her parents and brother always seemed keen to 'move on' – perhaps Asta needed a bit of time to get over it. Perhaps she needed to talk.

"I'm so sorry about Luna, Asta. Could you tell me a bit about her?" Lily sat carefully on the edge of the bed next to her. She touched the photo. "She's a beautiful husky."

"Elkhound," Asta corrected. "And I want to be alone."

Lily took a deep breath and remembered what her mother had said, about language barriers and people expressing themselves in different ways. She left Asta and decided that she would have to investigate for herself.

Just one more coffee first.

As she waited for the coffee to boil, Lily found a stack of tourist leaflets in a kitchen drawer. They advertised things to do in Tromsø, but one leaflet called '*Villmark*' ('Wilderness') caught her eye. It had a picture of a reindeer on the front. She opened it out. Inside, there was all sorts of information on guided treks to see walrus, reindeer and whales. It was a start – a really good start. There may not have been enough colour to compete with 'A Sky of Parrots', but 'Where the Reindeer Live' or 'Sea of Giants' were good titles. She had a feeling that, with a bit of luck, the Young Photographer of the Year competition could be back on!

Lily called her parents and left messages on their phones, begging them to book her on a wilderness trek. Her dad sent back a message saying he was in a meeting, but he added a big smiley face and a thumbs-up.

There was nothing left to do now until the others got home. Grabbing some gear from the cupboard, Lily got ready for some ski practice in the garden. Tomorrow she might end up on a trek, and she wouldn't want to get left behind. She wanted to be skiing right up front, with a view of everything.

She skied up and down the garden until she got her confidence back. She learned to turn and stop. She even managed a 'duckwalk' – nothing good enough to show Morten, but she was proud of herself for trying. She definitely felt happier. And she hadn't noticed before how the snow sparkled like tiny diamonds in the sun. It was as if she were in the middle of a glittery snow globe.

Chapter 7

Lily chose cheese to go with her flatbread. She'd already had muesli, and toast and jam. Linn came over with the coffee pot.

"I'll have another one," Lily said, raising her cup. She was really starting to like the taste.

"That's the last one," her mother said. "You'll never sleep!"

"That's the whole point. I don't want to be sleepy. I have to be wide awake to see the whales."

Ivan gripped her shoulder and shook it in a friendly manner. "My friend tells me there are lots of whales in the fjords right now. They come to fill up on fish before swimming all the way back to the Caribbean." He reached for a plate of pink salmon and tried to scoop some on to Lily's plate. "Perhaps you should be like the whales and eat fish, too."

"No thanks," Lily laughed. "Maybe tomorrow."

Ivan grinned. "There may not be a tomorrow. There are killer whales out there. One might jump up and … bite you!"

"There are orcas?" Lily's eyes widened. She briefly imagined a large photograph on a wall with her name next it. Title: 'Killers of Norway'. Her mum was watching her across the table with a big smile, as if she knew what she was thinking. She reached over and placed a hand on Lily's.

"Why don't you relax for the morning?" she said. "We have meetings, but we will be back at around midday. And then off to the Wilderness Centre! Be ready, and make sure you wrap up warmly."

"Time to start the day!" Ivan said, thumping the table again. Lily realised that it was just something he did to get things going.

"I look forward to hearing about your adventure, Lily," he said. "Maybe tonight, when you get back, we can have some *gløgg* and story-telling time. *Ja?*"

"*Ja!*" Lily repeated.

Linn entered the kitchen, shaking her head with despair. "Asta is still miserable."

"And *skikjøring*? Will she race tomorrow?" Ivan asked, his good mood vanishing. Linn shrugged. Ivan thumped the table again, but this time it was in anger.

Lily's parents quickly finished their coffee and gathered their things.

"See you at midday, Lily," her father said. "I'm looking forward to it."

"Me, too," Lily said with a grin. "I'm *really* looking forward to it."

"Oh, another thing …" Ivan turned in the doorway, his smile back in place. "There were elk at the edge of the forest this morning. You might be able to see them from the window in the study. Use the binoculars on the desk."

"Thank you, Ivan."

Linn and Morten began tidying up the breakfast plates. Lily helped, taking a sniff of the salmon before putting it in the fridge. Muesli and cheese and coffee was one thing, but fish was going too far! Morten saw her and laughed, but this time it was friendly, not cruel.

"It's good for you," he said. "Tomorrow, try it."

Lily wondered if maybe Morten was like his father; only patient with people who got on with life and tried new things.

Lily looked at her watch. It was two hours until her parents would be back. She had to prepare. Nothing could be allowed to go wrong – if a humpback whale flicked its tail or an orca surfaced with a white-cheeked grin, she was going to be ready to capture the perfect photo. She laid out all her camera pieces on the bed – zoom lens, cleaning cloth and extra battery pack. But even after going through everything three times, she still had plenty of time to spare.

Out of the study window, the forest at the end of the garden looked dark and mysterious. Somewhere inside it were elk. She picked up Ivan's binoculars and searched the tree line. There was nothing there now, but if she went to the bottom of the garden, perhaps she'd get a glimpse.

She popped her head around the living room door, where Linn was sitting surrounded by books.

"I'm going to practise skiing in the garden."

Linn smiled. "Good girl."

Lily grabbed her camera, shrugged on a coat and went outside, stopping first in the kitchen to pick up some food and drink. She grabbed biscuits and energy bars and took a flask of coffee in case she got cold and hungry waiting for the shy elk. If she saw them, perhaps she would have a photograph to enter into the competition after all. If she was lucky, she might have lots. Whales, orcas, eagles, seals … Norway was a pretty good destination for an adventurous young photographer, after all.

Chapter 8

Lily skied to the edge of the Larsens' land. She took the binoculars and peered into the forest. Nothing. The elk must have moved since the early morning sighting. *They might be hiding close behind a cluster of trees,* Lily thought. *It wouldn't hurt to venture into the forest just a little bit, would it?*

There had been no overnight snow, and the old ski trails were still there. Lily followed a track and pushed ahead quietly, looking left and right for animals. Occasionally, she saw pretty hares with bright white fur, but nothing else. She was starting to think the elk had moved on when, suddenly, the silence was pierced by a haunting scream. In *Wild Norway*, Lily had read that elk calls were like high-pitched howls. Excited, Lily headed towards the noise. It meant leaving the track and skiing on fresh snow, but she still had plenty of time.

After 15 minutes, she began to regret being so enthusiastic. She had started to ache, and the elk cries

40

were moving further away. Exhausted, she sat down next to a tree trunk and pulled an energy bar from her bag.

Everything was quiet.

She imagined the squawking of parrots and the noise of a jungle somewhere hot and dry. This was so different. But it was special, too. Who else could say they had been on holiday to a place where there was no noise – just sparkling snow, deep blue waters and shy creatures, some of them as big as buildings?

A rustle in the trees made her freeze. Lily twisted around.

There, standing just metres away, was a very small dog with grey fur. It looked up and Lily saw it right away – a heart-shaped mark between its eyes.

Luna! The naughty elkhound!

"Luna!" Lily called, but the dog moved away between the trees. "Luna!" Lily called again.

The dog disappeared, but she had to find it. Asta would be over the moon. Perhaps she'd even take part in the *skikjøring* race, and her dad would be happy, too. Lily was determined.

There was no way she could jump between trees and over roots in her skis, so she slipped them off and propped them against the tree. Then, running in her boots with her backpack over her shoulder, she went after Luna.

It was difficult to keep up – the dog moved from one place to another following scents, and Lily was clumsy in her ski boots. She tripped and fell, but each time she picked herself up and kept going. Her heart started to race with the effort and with worry. She was getting further away from the tracks, running deeper into the trees. What if she lost her way?

All I have to do is retrace my footprints, she told herself.
There was no need to stress; there wasn't any danger of being

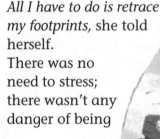

lost, and there was still plenty of time. Besides … she had just found Luna! The naughty puppy had stopped to sniff at something in the middle of a clearing, a wide area with no trees.

Lily got a biscuit from her bag and moved slowly towards her, saying, *"Kom da, kom da,"* – something she'd heard Morten say to Bodil. Luna looked up and trotted towards her. When the dog tried to grab the biscuit, Lily quickly hooked her finger through her collar and lifted the puppy up into her arms.

"Got you!" Lily panted. "I don't know what 'got you' is in Norwegian, but I've got you!"

Feeling victorious, and imagining what Asta looked like with a smile, she started back the way she'd come. Only, it began to get confusing. The footprints started to look like all the other lumps and bumps in the snow because of the uneven forest floor beneath it. And then there seemed to be no prints at all. She was lost.

There was no point in staying still, so she kept going forwards, hoping to pick up a track and, all the time, listening out for skiers who might help. But she heard only the crunch of her feet and her breathing, which had started to quicken. She walked for an hour perhaps, realising she must have been going in circles, and then the snow beneath her feet started to feel different. Softer. Looser.

There was a crack. The snow caved in a little.

Then WHOOSH! The forest floor collapsed and fell downwards, taking Lily and Luna with it.

Snow was everywhere – in her hair, eyes and mouth. It surrounded her like a cocoon. Where was she? She looked up to the surface from where she fell, high above her. She and Luna were at the bottom of a pit – a giant hole in the snow. She jumped up, but there was no solid ledge to hold on to. The soft snow just came away in her fingertips. She clawed at the sides of the pit, hoping to find tree roots or something that she could climb; but her arms and legs ached so much, and she was getting nowhere. She called and called, but the snow swallowed the sound and her throat began to hurt.

Sitting in the bottom of the hole, Lily cuddled Luna for warmth and wondered what to do.

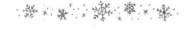

Hours went by. Hours of waiting for the sound of another human being …

Her parents would be home by now. They would be asking where she was. No one would know. They would be panicking, scared.

Lily gathered all her strength and shouted again and again, hoping she could crack the silence of the forest. But the only thing that cracked was her voice. It disappeared, and all she could manage was a whisper.

Luna started whimpering. The dog leaped out of her arms and began turning in circles at her feet.

"Shhh, Luna, quiet!" Luna's whining got louder and louder. Was she trying to say something? "Is someone coming, Luna? Are they going to rescue us?"

Lily couldn't call out, but she scooped up snow and threw it in the air, hoping to attract the passer-by. A crunch above. Movement. Snow drifted downwards. There was someone up there!

"Here! Here!" Lily rasped.

But it wasn't a human face that looked over the edge.

A huge cat with spotted fur and pointed ears stared down at her. Its mouth opened, revealing huge fangs.

Luna barked, but the cat wasn't scared. It reached its paw over the edge, violently clawing in the direction of Lily's face. Lily screamed for help, but her raw throat couldn't make any sound. She threw snow at it, and the cat leaped back. It paced above them, hissing.

It's going to jump, Lily thought. *It's going to jump and attack.*

There were no biscuits or energy bars left in her bag to throw. Only a flask. A flask of coffee … maybe that would work. Keeping her eyes on the cat above, Lily poured the coffee into the flask lid and threw the hot liquid up at the cat. It flinched and moved away. But it came back.

Lily didn't know what to do. She just kept throwing the coffee, but the cat didn't leave – and the coffee ran out … *Don't panic*, she told herself. *Don't panic*. But she was out of ammunition. There was only her camera, and what good was a camera? She could take a photo – perhaps the clicking sound would scare it away.

With the camera focused on the edge of the hole above, Lily's heart beat wildly as she waited for the big cat to return. It did. It was getting more confident, and this time it reached its paw so far down towards her, its back legs began slipping. If it fell into the pit with them there'd be no escape! Lily quickly took a photo. The automatic flash went off – a searing bright light – directly in the face of the animal.

The surprised cat let out a shriek and scrambled backwards.

And then there was nothing.

Luna stopped pacing and whining, and settled back down.

The cat was gone.

But the daylight was going, too. As the darkness closed in around her and the temperature started to drop, Lily held Luna tightly and cried.

Chapter 9

"Lily! Lily!"

At first, she thought the faint cries were in her imagination. But they called again. Lily jumped to her feet.

"Help!"

She yelled in desperation, swallowing down the soreness in her throat. It was no good. She had no voice, and nothing that might attract attention – no flare or whistle. How could she let them know she was here? Without a signal, the searchers might never come this deep into the woods, where the trees were tight together and skiing was impossible. They might miss her.

She pushed that thought from her mind. She also tried not to think of the big cat and the possibility that it would return – a hungry mother looking for food for her cubs wouldn't give up. A camera flash would only scare it for a little while …

Wait! The camera flash … She could make light!

Lily took the camera from its case and turned it on. The photo she had taken earlier came up on the screen. The picture was a bit blurred, but it was incredible and dramatic. The cat, with its sharp fangs, was reaching towards her, the bright light caught in its wild eyes … She may have missed the giants of the sea but she'd definitely have one photo to send into the competition. If she got out of there alive …

Pointing her camera through the hole in the snow above, Lily took picture after picture, triggering the flash over and over again. Each time, the snow around her became momentarily luminous, like a flashing beacon in the night. Anyone looking in her direction would see it, and so long as her battery lasted, she would keep trying.

FLASH!

FLASH!

FLASH!

Hundreds of times she pressed the button on the camera but no one came, and Lily watched in despair as the battery started to run down. She had ten, maybe 20 more chances. She couldn't waste them. She would wait for the right time, whenever that was.

Holding Luna tightly in her arms, she listened. Her teeth chattered with the cold.

"Lily!"

A call!

"Lily!"

Louder this time.

"Lily, where are you?"

There were lots of voices calling now. A whole search party of people.

"Lilyaaaaaaa!"

Now! Lily made the camera flash twice in a row to keep the snow lit up for longer, hoping a searcher would see.

"Over here! Over here!"

Yes! She flashed the camera again … and then it wouldn't work anymore. The battery was dead. Would it be enough?

Minutes passed by and Lily was filled with despair. Perhaps they hadn't seen the light at all, but spotted something in the other direction – the movement of

a rabbit or fox. *How long would it be until they gave up?* wondered Lily. Tears rolled down her cheeks as she gasped over and over, trying to make a sound. Then, suddenly, she saw light above her. Beams criss-crossed in the sky. Torches. She threw snow in the air as high as she could, making a shower that she hoped would catch the light.

"Lily!" Her mother's voice.

"Stop! It's a snowdrift!"

The voice was Ivan's. He then said something in Norwegian and there was a discussion. They were so close, so close … Then her father's voice.

"If it's Lily, why isn't she saying anything?"

"She may be too thirsty or tired," Morten's voice said. "We think she fell in deep snow. We are working out how to spread our weight so we don't fall."

Lily could have cried with relief. *Thank you, Morten!*

There was more discussion and then shuffling. A slithering sound on the snow above her. Bright torchlight hit her eyes. The torch carrier stared, yelling. She was found!

"Come on, Luna, this is it!" Lily whispered, zipping up the tiny puppy in her backpack. She put the backpack on and felt the puppy wriggle. "Don't worry, little one. You're going home."

The man with the torch leaped down into the snowy hole with her. She didn't know him, and he didn't smile. Without a word, he began to wrap rope around her middle and between her legs, creating a harness.

He called to the people above and the rope tightened and jolted her. The man lifted her up as high as he could. She grabbed a hand that was reaching for her from above. It was Ivan. All the search torches were pointed at him.

"*Jeg har deg,*" he said. "I've got you."

"Thank you, Ivan," Lily whispered. "*Takk, Ivan. Takk.*"

"It's okay. Now, when I pull you up, you must lie flat on the snow like me," he said. "We need to spread our weight or the snow will collapse again."

Lily saw he was lying flat, his arms and legs stretched out like a starfish. The search party were standing at the edge of the clearing, holding ropes that were attached to Ivan's ankles.

Lily could hear her parents crying with relief as she was pulled from the drift. Ivan told her to ignore them and keep her eyes on him. She nodded and, remembering what he had said, lay as flat as she could on the snow. The search group pulled the ropes and, together, Ivan and Lily were dragged back across the snow to the safety of the trees, where people were waiting with blankets and hot drinks. And her mother and father gave her a hug that went on forever.

It was early evening, but outside the sky was pitch black. Only an hour before, Lily had been stuck in a hole, fearing for her life. Now, after a medical check-up, she was sitting in front of a fire with a glass of *gløgg* in her hand. Her mother and father smiled at her across the room. She wanted to sit with them, but she had two new friends who wouldn't leave her side, Luna and Asta, who – it turned out – owned an amazing smile.

"You are my hero!" Asta said, topping up Lily's glass of *gløgg*.

"But I am surprised your teachers don't tell you about how pressure works," Ivan said, shaking his head. "If you take your skis off, it's obvious your weight will—,"

"Stop it, Ivan," Linn tutted. "Lily did not have time to think about science. She was rescuing Luna. And she showed a lot of common sense, using her camera to get attention."

"Pretty clever," Morten said. "What made you think of it?"

Lily's voice was too whispery to explain, so she passed over her camera. Morten's face dropped. He looked up and around at everyone in the room with wide eyes. "A lynx."

"A lynx?" Ivan reached out his hand for the camera, and it was passed around until everyone had seen.

"How? What happened?" Linn said, but Lily had no voice. They would have to wait for the story.

Chapter 10

When Lily woke, Asta was sitting at the foot of her bed with Luna on her lap.

"You only have one day left," she said brightly. "What do you want to do?"

"I want you to show me your life, Asta," Lily said with a sleepy smile.

"Great. We have lots to do. Come." Asta thumped the bed and Lily laughed. She was so much like her father!

Breakfast was already laid out, and just the smell of coffee cured Lily's sleepiness. After the adventure of the day before, she had slept like a log all night.

"What will the hero have today?" Ivan said with twinkling eyes.

"The full Norwegian breakfast, please!"

Ivan's eyebrows shot up. "Even the fish?"

"Yes, even the fish. Got to try everything!"

Ivan banged the table. "Yes! That's my girl."

"She's my girl," Lily's dad said, banging the table, too.

"She's mine!" Asta said, joining in. Everybody laughed.

"So, what have you got planned today?" Ivan drummed his fingers on the table top.

"I want to take Lily to the log cabin," Asta said. "Perhaps take the boat out. We can go by ourselves. We'll be fine."

"Oh no," Linn said, wagging her finger. "I think we have had enough adventure."

"And the race this afternoon …" Ivan folded his arms across his chest and looked at his daughter expectantly. "It decides who goes through to the finals."

"Maybe. Maybe not." Asta shrugged and looked the other way. Lily wondered if she was winding her father up on purpose.

"Be a loser if you want," he said. His eyes twinkled.

"Will they be okay, going to the cabin on their own?" Lily's mother said. She was worried.

Linn patted her arm. "In Norway, children are free to explore. It helps them get good at making the right decisions. They will be totally fine. The cabin is just down the road. A very short distance."

Lily's mum bit her lip, but she nodded. Asta clapped her hands.

"Come on, Lily, eat that fish and let's go."

Happy Asta was great fun, and they laughed all the way to the cabin. It was a wooden hut raised on stilts, jutting over the water.

"It's a boat shed," Asta explained. "But we have blankets and games in there, too. It's like a playhouse. I called my friends. They're already here to meet you."

Inside, a girl and a boy were playing cards on a blanket on the floor.

"This is Britt and Erik," Asta said, pointing in turn to the girl and boy.

"*Hei!*" They waved.

"You have to speak in English," Asta told them. "They are not as good as me, though," she added, proudly.

"That's okay. My Norwegian is really bad," Lily said shyly.

"What words do you know?" said Erik.

"None."

"Yeah, that is really bad!" Britt laughed. Lily laughed, too. She knew that this was just how they spoke.

Wrapped in patchwork blankets and eating spiced cookies baked by Britt, they chatted while Erik played Norwegian pop songs on his guitar.

"Do you know any Norwegian pop stars?" he asked Lily.

"Abba?"

He blew a raspberry. "No, Abba was from Sweden! Norway's most famous band was A-ha! The lead singer was called Morten."

"Like your brother!" Lily said to Asta.

She rolled her eyes. "He hates it when people say that ... So, say it, okay! It will be so funny."

They sang some more. Then they played, '*Idioten*', – a crazy game where they shouted at each other, slammed cards on the floor and laughed until they felt sick. When they'd finished, Britt and Erik seemed keen to find out everything they could about Lily, and didn't stop asking questions about her life and her hobbies. They even asked why Lily had chosen to have a holiday in Norway, and she had to explain all about her photography and her cancelled trip to South Africa.

"I feel sorry for you," Erik said. "South Africa would be an amazing country to see."

"I was a bit sad at first," Lily said carefully. She didn't want to upset them. "But only because I wanted to see a sky full of parrots."

"There isn't much to see here," Britt said, shaking her head. "No parrots."

"But you have whales and seals and elk," Lily said quickly. "And how many people get to meet a lynx!"

Asta looked at her watch. "We go! *Vi sees!*" Asta said to the others. "It means 'See you later'," she told Lily.

"*Vi sees,* Erik and Britt!" Lily said.

They left the cosy cabin and went back outside into the white world.

"Is that true, that you were sad to come to Norway?" Asta asked.

"Yes, but I was being silly. Adventure is where you look for it. And I found it, didn't I? I'm happy now. Really, I am."

Asta nodded. "I am sorry you did not get your parrot sky."

It was harder going up the slope back to the house, but Lily enjoyed the achy feeling in her muscles – it meant she was getting stronger – and she felt a little

sad that this funny way of life, with its cross-country skiing and crazy breakfasts and card games with friends, would soon be over.

At the ski rack outside the house, Asta stamped her foot in the snow.

"You are right," she said abruptly. "We should make adventures wherever we are. This afternoon I am going *skikjøring*. You will come and watch me?"

"Absolutely, Asta. I would love to."

"Great. We hurry."

Chapter 11

Lily stood with her parents and the Larsens near the finish line. The starting line was out of sight. It was a shame not to send Asta off with a cheer, but Ivan said it was the cheering at the end that counted – when they were tired and wanting to slow down, it gave a little bit of extra support – a push to get them over the finish line.

There were shouts in the distance as the group set off, and the whoops got louder and louder as the skiers got closer. Within minutes, they could be seen. A pack of skiers led by dogs. From afar, they looked like a herd of stampeding animals.

"She is in third place," Ivan said, lowering his binoculars. "Bodil is perhaps too old now."

"Bodil is still good," Morten said, nudging his father. "You'll see."

People around began to whoop and clap and call the names of people they knew in the race, encouraging them to push harder and go fast. The jingle of cheering bells on the cold air filled Lily with a feeling she couldn't describe – it was excitement and enjoyment, but something extra … She felt alive. Yes, this was life!

An idea struck her, and Lily crouched down at the edge of the finish line. She took the camera from her case and attached the right lens. She held it in position, keeping her hand steady, waiting for the shot she had in her mind.

Cheers suddenly burst from the crowd around her. Lily held her camera tightly and watched the approaching racers like a hawk; she couldn't miss the moment. Then, Morten's voice – loud and proud: "Asta! *Ja!*" – gave her the cue she needed.

She was coming. Lily held her breath.

There! Bodil's face came into view. Behind him, Asta. Her limbs were working hard, and she was pushing with her poles to get every last drop of speed. Powdered snow flew around their feet like clouds. Lily clicked; she carried on clicking until Asta had passed the finish line.

"Fantastic, Asta! Fantastic!" Lily said, running to her side.

Asta doubled over, panting. There was a sparkle in her eyes and a huge smile across her face.

"I was second place. Enough to get through to the finals. It's great."

"We should go home and drink some *gløgg* now," Lily said. "You need to rest."

"Actually, we don't have time, do we, Pappa?"

Lily turned around. The Larsens and her parents were standing behind her. After giving his daughter a huge hug, Ivan looked at his watch.

"No – it should be happening at—," Ivan stopped himself from giving too much away. "No time. We should hurry now. Lily, pack your camera. You are coming with us."

"Where are we going?"

Lily's parents shrugged and smiled. A surprise.

"Aren't you coming?" Lily reached for her mother.

"We'll see you back at the house," she smiled. "Go on, have fun."

"And Morten?"

"He will deal with Asta's race details. There is paperwork."

"A-ha!" Lily said. Morten stopped and looked at her.

"What did you say?"

"Nothing. Just 'A-ha'!"

"Asta, you told her about the pop group? I'll get you back for this."

Lily got into the back of Ivan's car with Asta, both of them laughing at Morten's embarrassment. Then she was overcome with tiredness. After a few minutes, the soft Norwegian voices and the movement of the car rocked her to sleep.

Hands wrapped around her eyes.

"What's going on?"

"Shhh!" It was Asta's voice. "I'm making sure you can't see. It's a surprise. You need to get out of the car, but don't look, okay? Keep your eyes shut."

Lily edged along the back seat to the door, eyes squeezed tight. She felt her way out of the car and stood in the cold night air. The atmosphere felt different here – breezier, colder. The smell of the sea.

"We are in Hillesøya," Asta said. "We are at the edge of the Norwegian Sea."

"Can I look?"

"Wait just a moment. When I count to three, I want you to look up. Ready? *En, to, tre* … Look up!"

Lily looked up.

In the darkness, moving swirls of electric green flickered across the sky.

"What is that?" she gasped.

"The Northern Lights."

The green waves stretched and shimmered above them, their edges fluttering purple and blue like a dance. It reflected on the still water below, and it was impossible to tell where the sea ended and the sky began. Lily didn't even think to get her camera from its case. She stood, mesmerised, in total wonder. A tear ran down her cheek.

"What do you think?" Asta whispered.

"It's, it's …" Lily shook her head. "It's beautiful. It's amazing."

Asta swept the tear from Lily's cheek with her thumb.

"It's your parrot sky, Lily. I wanted you to have your parrot sky."

Chapter 12

Lily walked through the exhibition with a flutter in her heart.

"This one's good." Her father leaned forward to read the information page. "It's a pod of orcas off the coast of Canada ..." He ruffled Lily's hair. "I'm sorry you didn't get to see them for yourself, darling. But I suppose there wouldn't have been room in the competition for two orca photographs."

The standard this year was excellent. There were lizards shedding skins, camel trains trekking the desert, Thai monks in meditation. Snapshots of life from across the globe. Lily never expected to be up there with them, but there she was.

Her photograph.

The display wall was covered in dark cloth, and the stark white image on it looked larger than life. Lily blushed when she saw it.

Lily's mother, glowing with pride, took her hand and pulled her forwards.

"Come. Read it for yourself."

> Skikjøring – Girl and Dog
>
> Photographer: Liliana Costas, age 11
>
> Location: Tromsø, Norway
>
> 2nd Place

Lily was smiling so hard her face began to ache. She clapped a hand over her mouth in case other people noticed.

"Are you sorry you didn't enter the lynx photograph?"

"No, it wasn't in focus. A winning photograph has to be technically perfect. And besides, I don't think the photographer should be part of the story. A photographer's role is to observe life, you know."

"Beautifully put, Lily."

"And we're very glad this photographer's role wasn't to be a big cat's dinner ... So, what's the prize?" asked her father.

"A new camera – top of the range. First prize was a safari trip to Kenya. I don't mind, though," she added. "I really don't."

"Your time will come. Maybe sooner than you think." He smiled warmly and put his hand on her shoulder. "Aunty Agda is getting impatient to see us. So, would next autumn be okay?"

"You're kidding me!" Lily said. "Thank you, thank you! Although, I wouldn't have changed Norway for the world."

"You should call Asta and let her know," Lily's mother said.

Lily stepped closer to the picture and looked at her friend's face, pink with exertion. She and Bodil were in perfect focus, standing out, crisp as a Norwegian day.

Lily hoped memories of her time in Norway would always stay as fresh as the snow – even the not-so-good ones, like tripping up the cross-country skiers, falling into a snowdrift and fighting off a lynx. But she knew one experience would shine more brightly than the others – the one where she stood with her incredible Norsk friend and watched the dance of the Northern Lights – her very own parrot sky.

Now answer the questions …

1 Which country did Lily expect to be visiting at the start of the story?

2 What breed of dog is Luna?

3 Can you find an example of a simile on page 15?

4 How would you describe Asta's character before Lily finds Luna? How did Ivan feel about the lost puppy? Find some words and phrases in the text to support your opinion.

5 Can you explain how Lily felt when she realised she had become lost in the forest?

6 Give three examples from the story to show how Lily begins to adapt to the Norwegian way of life over the course of her holiday.

7 Did it matter that neither Lily nor Asta won the competitions they entered? Were either of them unhappy about coming second? Use evidence from the text to support your answer.

8 Like Lily, have you ever had to do something you didn't want to, and been surprised by how much you enjoyed it?

all the cousins I am sure you and Robert will provide for them!"

Yes, all Meg's dreams were coming true and she truly felt no couple could possibly be as happy as she and David.

But several rows further back in the Castle Chapel sat a husband and wife who would have disagreed with her.

Fergus and Heather Lyall, resplendent in their new clothes, Fergus's red hair blazing just like a torch above his dark blue jacket and Glentorran kilt, were certain that *they* were the happiest people in the whole wide world.

In London, on their behalf, the Duke had sold the diamond brooch that Mrs. Van Ashton had so generously given Fergus and with the proceeds a new modern fishing-boat had been purchased.

The *Lady Viola* now floated proudly in Glentorran harbour and Fergus knew his little son would have a future to inherit if he chose to follow his father's occupation.

*

Waiting impatiently at the altar the Duke was aware of nothing but the thudding of his heart.

The organ was playing, but he could not have told what the tune was.

Then the music changed completely as he heard the congregation rise to their feet.

Turning round, he watched in humble amazement as a vision in white silk and a cloudy chiffon veil studded with small silver stars floated down the aisle towards him.

Viola's bouquet cascaded from her gloved hands – a riot of white lilies and pink carnations and, there nestling between them, a few buds of the white and pink rose called *Grace Darling* she had admired so much in the Glentorran gardens all those weeks ago.

Only old Angus McAndrew knew the long hours he had laboured, nursing his rose bushes inside the glasshouse so he could provide the blooms she wanted on this special day.

And behind Viola, holding up the end of her long silk train came one solitary pageboy, red-headed Ian Lyall, so proud of his tiny kilt and sporran that he could hardly breathe.

Viola turned to smile affectionately at her twin who was giving her away.

He winked at her with brotherly good humour as he gently placed her hand onto the Duke's arm.

Together they turned to face the Minister and as the solemn words rang out for everybody to hear, Lady Viola Northcombe became the Duchess of Glentorran.

She lifted back her veil and gazed up in adoration at the man she loved so much.

He bent to kiss her and as his lips touched hers, she knew with every fibre of her being that their love was a gift from God and thus Eternal.

They both felt that their souls were being lifted to the stars as an angelic choir sang the praises of their love.

"You have always had my love and my heart. Now you possess my very soul – for ever and ever in this world and the next," Robert whispered to her.

And Viola knew that her new life in the *Castle of Dreams* would indeed be Heaven itself.